Ma

Castles and
Knights

written by Deborah Murrell
illustrated by Sue Hendra and Paul Linnet

consultant: Christopher Gravett

A catalogue record for this book is available from the British Library

Published by Ladybird Books Ltd
80 Strand London WC2R 0RL
A Penguin Company

2 4 6 8 10 9 7 5 3 1
© LADYBIRD BOOKS LTD MMVIII. This edition MMXII

ISBN: 978-0-71819-590-8

Printed in China

Contents

Some words appear in **bold** in this book.
Turn to the glossary to learn about them.

What is a castle?

Castles were the homes of kings and **nobles**. They were built to protect the people who lived in them from attack. Most castles were built between the **9th and 16th centuries**.

If enemies attacked, all the local people might move into the castle for safety. Castles had to be big enough for them all.

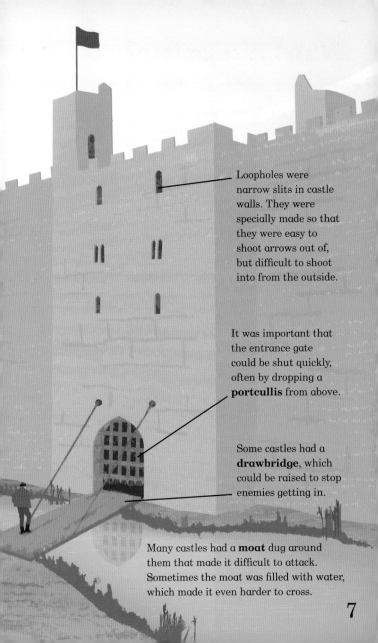

Loopholes were narrow slits in castle walls. They were specially made so that they were easy to shoot arrows out of, but difficult to shoot into from the outside.

It was important that the entrance gate could be shut quickly, often by dropping a **portcullis** from above.

Some castles had a **drawbridge**, which could be raised to stop enemies getting in.

Many castles had a **moat** dug around them that made it difficult to attack. Sometimes the moat was filled with water, which made it even harder to cross.

7

Early castles

The very first castles were made of wood. The simplest ones were called 'ringworks'. These were fenced areas surrounded by a ditch. Motte and bailey castles were the next step up from this.

The fenced bailey, or yard, contained houses and barns for animals and food.

The motte was a mound of earth that usually had a watchtower on the top. It was used to spot enemies coming from a long way away. If the motte was big enough, the main house might be built on it, too.

Motte and bailey castle

Wood was easy to find, and quick to build with. However, wooden castles could easily be burnt down. So, soon, rich people began to build their castles in stone.

Who lived there?

The lords who lived in castles with their families usually also had soldiers living with them for protection, and staff to cook and clean for them. The village peasants would have lived outside the castle.

Locked up!

Prisoners were usually locked up in the tower or **keep**, called 'donjon' in French. This is where the word 'dungeon' comes from.

Some castles had an 'oubliette', a very small space where a prisoner was kept until he died of hunger or thirst. Some oubliettes were in a tunnel that led to the sea or castle moat. Prisoners could either stay there or jump into the water to drown!

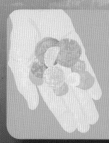

Some captured nobles were held to **ransom**. They were usually treated well and released as soon as their families paid the money demanded.

Castle life

The great hall was the main room of a castle, where people would eat, talk and be entertained. A noble family had their own bedrooms, but everyone else often had to sleep on the floor together. There were also kitchens, store rooms for food and even a chapel to pray in.

Nobles enjoyed feasts of meat, fish, fruit and nuts. Water was often so dirty that no one wanted to drink it. Instead, people drank ale. Nobles drank wine, too.

Many castles had a court jester, as well as musicians who entertained the family and their guests.

Castle toilets were very simple, and more than one person might use them at once. They were usually just a hole in the floor that emptied through passages in the walls. In one castle siege, the attackers broke in by climbing up the toilet shaft!

The only heat in castles came from open fires, and servants had to wash outside the castle in a river or moat, which would have been very cold!

13

Under siege

It was difficult to attack a stone castle. Firstly, the land around it would have to be captured, and then the castle surrounded until the owner surrendered. This was called a **siege**.

A catapult called a mangonel was used to throw rocks and other objects

Siege engines were special machines used for attacking a castle.

Another siege engine was a tall tower on wheels with soldiers inside. This tower was rolled up to a castle wall so that the soldiers could fight the castle defenders and try to get in over the top.

A siege could be a very slow way of capturing a castle, so armies might also attack the castle walls or its soldiers to speed up the process!

If you have a computer, you can download posters of different castles and knights from www.ladybird.com/madabout

Fighting knights

Knights were soldiers on horseback who fought for the king or the lord above them in **rank**. In return, they were given money, or land to farm and build on.

Mail armour   **Plate armour**

Most knights wore mail for protection. This was made of thousands of tiny, linked metal rings. Plate armour, made from solid sheets of metal, began to be worn in the 15th century, but was very heavy and expensive.

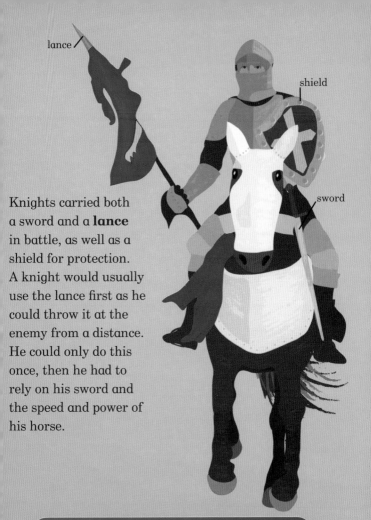

lance

shield

sword

Knights carried both
a sword and a **lance**
in battle, as well as a
shield for protection.
A knight would usually
use the lance first as he
could throw it at the
enemy from a distance.
He could only do this
once, then he had to
rely on his sword and
the speed and power of
his horse.

Horses, armour and weapons were expensive,
so knights needed to be rich men to afford
them. Horses were so valuable that they
sometimes also wore armour to protect them!

17

Knight school

To become a knight, a young noble boy would have to leave home to be trained when he was around seven years old. He would serve a lord and lady as a **page**, and learn basic fighting skills and manners.

Pages often learnt to fight using wooden swords, and learned to ride on a wooden 'horse' as it was safer.

If a page was successful, he would become a squire (a knight's assistant) around the age of fourteen. A squire looked after a knight, and learnt more difficult fighting skills. By working hard, a squire could become a knight by the age of twenty-one.

To become a knight, a squire was 'dubbed'. This meant being tapped on the shoulders with a sword. Only another knight or the king or queen could do this.

In some countries, people can still be dubbed knights by the royal family. It is a very special honour.

Tournaments and jousting

To stay fit when they were not at war, knights fought each other in pretend battles, called tournaments. Although knights could still be injured, there were rules, such as having to use blunt lances, to make the competitions safer.

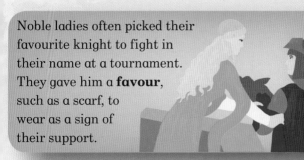

Noble ladies often picked their favourite knight to fight in their name at a tournament. They gave him a **favour**, such as a scarf, to wear as a sign of their support.

Jousting was a popular contest. Two knights charged at each other and tried to knock the other off his horse with a lance. If one succeeded, he got maximum points. But a knight could also get points for hitting the other knight's shield, and for breaking his own lance!

21

Heraldry

When they were in full armour, it was difficult to tell one knight from another. Knights began to wear symbols on their shields and armour so that they could be recognized.

Heralds, who carried messages in battle, had to be very good at remembering the different symbols. They soon had a system for recognizing someone by their **coat of arms.** This system is still around today, and is called heraldry.

Herald

Heraldry has its own language to describe the different colours and patterns used on coats of arms.

Objects displayed on a shield are called 'charges'.

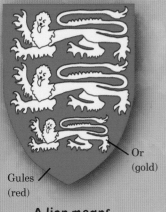

Or
(gold)

Gules
(red)

**A lion means
'courage'**

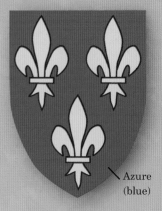

Azure
(blue)

**The fleur-de-lys is
a symbol of France**

Simple shapes on a shield are called 'ordinaries'.

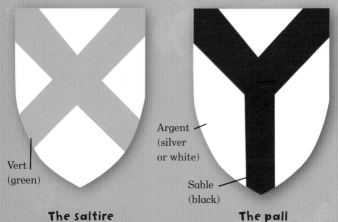

Vert
(green)

The saltire

Argent
(silver
or white)

Sable
(black)

The pall

23

Battles and crusades

During a battle, both knights on warhorses and foot soldiers fought alongside each other.

Foot soldiers stood at the front of the battle and held sharp weapons such as **pikes**. These were dangerous to the enemy knights and horses charging towards them.

Knights charged at each other and also tried to break up the lines of enemy foot soldiers. On horseback, they could do a lot of damage with their heavy swords.

The Holy Land is a part of the Middle East that is important to Muslims, Christians and Jews. During the 11th century, new Muslim rulers took over the land and it became dangerous for Christians to visit.

Christian fighters called the Muslim army the 'Saracens'

The Pope asked the Christians to lead a crusade, or holy war, against these rulers. There were nine wars over the next two hundred years, and many lives were lost.

25

Fantastic facts

- Many castles had more than one line of walls. If the attackers got past the first wall, they were faced with a second or even a third!

- The **gatehouse** at Caernarfon castle in Wales had five doors and six portcullises, making it very hard to break in to.

- Knights had to obey a set of rules for polite behaviour. This was called chivalry. Rules included being brave and fair in battle, treating prisoners well and being polite to noble ladies.

- A rich knight often had several horses. He rode a warhorse in battles and tournaments. For everyday riding he had a lighter horse, and for carrying his baggage he would have used a packhorse.

- Murder holes were holes in the floor of a gatehouse. People defending the castle could drop rocks, boiling water, oil or anything they liked from them onto the enemy!

- Many castles had a well inside the castle walls. This meant that they had water to drink even when they were under siege.

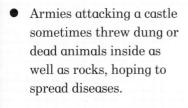

- Armies attacking a castle sometimes threw dung or dead animals inside as well as rocks, hoping to spread diseases.

- The invention of guns and gunpowder in the 14th century slowly changed the ways of fighting for good. Castles were not strong enough to stand up to **cannon** fire and even a knight's armour couldn't protect him from bullets. By the end of the **Middle Ages**, knights' special skills were no longer needed and many castles fell into ruins.

27

Amazing awards

Best defences

Caerphilly Castle in Wales has two lines of walls and is surrounded by a huge lake made by damming a stream.

Largest castle

The largest castle still standing is Hradcany Castle in Prague, Czech Republic. It covers 570x130 metres, which makes it bigger than a football stadium.

Most beautiful

Neuschwanstein was built to look like a fairy tale castle, with many beautiful towers and spires. It is in the mountains of Bavaria, Germany and is visited by over one million people each year.

Most famous knight

The most famous knight of all is probably Sir Lancelot, King Arthur's favourite knight. However, he was not real, but a character from a French poem!

Oldest castle

Doué-la-Fontaine Castle, in France, has probably the oldest known stone keep, or 'donjon'. It dates from around 950 AD.

Furthest north

Kajaani Castle, in Finland, is the most northern castle in the world. It was destroyed in 1717 during the Great Nordic War. Only the ruins are left.

Glossary

cannon – a large, heavy gun.

coat of arms – symbols on armour or flags, used to represent a family or country.

drawbridge – a bridge that could be raised or lowered.

favour – (or token) something a lady gave a knight to show that she supported him.

gatehouse – a room over the gate of a city or castle.

keep – a tower with thick stone walls that was the most protected part of a castle.

lance – a long, pointed weapon that was usually thrown in battle.

moat – a deep trench, often filled with water, that was dug around a castle for protection.

nobles – people born into rich or powerful families.

page – a boy training to become a knight.

pike – a long, pointed weapon used for stabbing at enemies.

portcullis – a gate in a castle made of wood or metal that could be lowered quickly.

rank – a person's place in society.

ransom – money paid for a prisoner to be set free.

siege – the surrounding of a city or castle by enemy forces.

Years	Century
0-100	1st century
100-200	2nd century
200-300	3rd century
300-400	4th century
400-500	5th century
500-600	6th century
600-700	7th century
700-800	8th century
800-900	9th century
900-1000	10th century
1000-1100	11th century
1100-1200	12th century
1200-1300	13th century
1300-1400	14th century
1400-1500	15th century
1500-1600	16th century
1600-1700	17th century
1700-1800	18th century
1800-1900	19th century
1900-2000	20th century
2000-2100	21st century

The Middle Ages spans 700-1300 (8th to 13th century).

Century guide